Redeeming the Time

How to Recover from Setbacks

By Linda C. Sanders

Printed in the United States of America

First Printing, 2018

Emerge Publishing Group
1491 S Sunnylane Road
Del City, OK 73115

www.emergepublishing.com

I dedicate this book to you, Lord.
The work of the Holy Spirit in
my Life.

Table of Contents

FOREWORD

From the Inner Circle

As I'm writing this foreword, I'm sitting amid years of hard work, dedication, sacrifice, love, and support from my Mother, Linda Collette Sanders. It is with great honor that I write this foreword to share with you the impact of the book you are holding in your hands. It is a life work that culminated during a time of setback and reflection. Through the hands of my Mother, you will be guided through setbacks and come out on the other side, restored, replenished, and refreshed.

Here are a few things to keep in mind as you read. This is a redemptive story that tells of the redeeming love of God.

This is a compelling story, that will capture your heart, and touch you deep in your soul.

This is a transforming story that will literally take you from a place of despair and despondency to a place of freedom and liberty.

This is our story! The words penned by my Mother are from her heart. Deep within the recesses of her soul, she shares her experience; but it is our (yours and mine) experience.

Be set free and be reminded that now is the time! Redeeming the time begins with one step and then another. Let's take the walk together.

Welcome to the journey of the redeemed life!

Kelly Ramsey
The Eldest Daughter of Mama's Inner Circle

INTRODUCTION

We cannot stay on the ground. We won't survive. We must redeem the time for the days are evil. Redemption is God's plan for the earth. We must stop and assess, which is self-examination, and continue. But, first we must recognize if we are stuck or delayed in a time which is the result of an interruption or setback in our lives that prevents us from fulfilling God's plan and purpose..

What does God's redemption for us look like? Why is it necessary?

Let's remember that He did not leave us without a Seer. It is the Holy Spirit.

When the enemy comes in like a flood, He will lift a standard which allows us to get unstuck and continue the path of God's purpose for us. Evilness is running rampant in the earth. It can come in the form of interruptions and can escalate into setbacks in our life. Interruptions can break in upon us and cut us off, stop or obstruct our visions and the path we're on to fulfill that vision. The setback is a delay and can return us to an earlier time and further delay our Kairos moment.

The word Kairos is a Greek word which means opportune time (Kairos), opportunity; however, implies not the convenience of the season, but the necessity of the task at hand whether the time provides a good, convenient opportunity or not. These are times at which certain foreordained events take place or necessary accomplishments need to take place.

It is our responsibility to redeem the time. How do we do that?

We must be open to the direction of the Holy Spirit. God's redemption plan for mankind is already established. Jesus

Christ paid the price for our redemption. Our part is to continue with the vision and plans God has given each one of us. We don't want to leave this earth without fulfilling our God-given instructions.

The Value of Interruptions

I was blessed to have an interruption in my life. It taught me what a marriage vow meant. After 45 years of marriage, my husband transitioned to be with the Lord. It was in that moment that I realized I was living out a marital vow: for richer or poorer, in sickness and in health, till death do us part. It gave me an opportunity to apply Godly principles to my life without being aware of it. Our words are powerful. Death and life is in the power of the tongue; even if you don't have a full understanding of what you are saying.

An example can be given in Genesis 11:6 on the power of oneness when men purposed to build a tower. It's called the Tower of Babel in the City of Babel. The Lord looked down and saw that they were as one and purposed to build a tower unto heaven. The point is when you are joined as one, nothing is impossible to achieve. It is in a marriage covenant, where God is in the middle, it's established. As with men and women, we can get in disobedience and break covenant. But the principles of that covenant are still established and we learn from our errors and correction by God.

The sudden departure of my husband was my Tsunami. Other tremors and challenges led up to this interruption; but, it prompted me to complete the writing of this book, Redeeming the Time - *How to Recover from Setbacks*. The intent and purpose of this book is not to take you to the valley without bringing you back up to the top of the mountain for instructions.

We can be stuck or delayed in natural development stages of our lives: childhood, adolescence, young adult or more mature stages. Don't make light of interruptions in life. There is a clear path to recovery. The first step is to acknowledge that we need a seer to lead and guide us back to recovery; the second is to devise a plan on how to recover from upheavals in life; the third is to recognize recovery is a process; fourth, be aware of the signposts towards recovery and finally, redeem the time and be confident you will gain the time.

Chapter 1

HOW TO RECOVER FROM UPHEAVALS IN THIS LIFE AND REGAIN CONTROL AFTER A SUDDEN CHANGE OR DISRUPTION

My husband, Albert, was diagnosed with Pancreatic Cancer – Stage IV in September 2010 and made his transition in February 2011. We had no warning of the gravity of his condition prior to that time. He had been diagnosed with congestive heart failure in 2008 and had been in treatment for that condition. Prior to these two conditions, he had retired after 40 years, in 2002, because of a back condition. In all, his physical challenges were from 2002 through 2011 after his retirement. His illnesses were not life threatening at that point.

Our journey began in 2004, when the need arose for us to assist his 93-year-old grandmother who was living alone. We moved to San Francisco to care for her. In the process, my husband's medical challenges increased. His blood pressure was uncontrollable which accelerated and contributed to his congestive heart condition. On this journey, his medical condition was misdiagnosed and we were just on the verge of changing our medical facilities when in September 2009, we were given an accurate diagnosis of Albert's condition.

It was there Albert's diagnosis of pancreatic cancer stage IV was given. The emergency room physician shared with both of us that we were getting ready to experience things that would change our lives. This was our great Tsunami. After my husband's departure in 2011, I returned to writing this book, Redeeming the Time - *How to Recover from Setbacks*. Until that time, I didn't have the last part to continue my writing journey. I trust this book will assist others who are or will be going through similar situations that disrupt their lives.

What do you do when your hero departs you've known your entire life, your Mom. And then two years later, your covenant partner for over 45 years, your husband departs.

I asked the Holy Spirit to reveal truth to me. And he did. I had an unplanned conversation with my sister, who is two years younger than me. We were talking about influences in our lives. Specifically, our husbands and mother. Both of us were and have been married over 35 years. We agreed that our mother influenced our perspective and roles as wives and mothers. Both of us, with a little variation, have put husbands first. Our Mom's philosophy, because of their generation, was that you continue in a marriage for various reasons; mainly because of the children. And for the institution of marriage.

Our paths were different in marriage; but, we reached the same vantage point. My philosophy on divorce is that no matter how long you have been married, in reality, you divorce many times without filing the legal documents to end the marriage. Divorce is attempting to sever relational ties. A friend described her divorce as having your arm pulled out of its socket. I believe my marriage was rooted and grounded in love and God in the center. The quirks in 45 years of marriage had to be worked out by the two of us with the help of the Holy Ghost.

The departure of my mother and my husband were major. I pondered at times, what good things came out of their early departure from my life. Reflecting on the past is necessary at times. But, you cannot stay there. That's how you stay stuck. In looking back, their departure enabled me to recognize God's hand on my life and I'm still here with a sound mind because of his grace.

And still functioning in my other roles as a mom, grandmother, sibling and a close friend to those who believe in me.

Realistically, I recognize now that at that time I felt abandoned at the doorstep of my life. How do you squeeze a full-grown woman into a basket and leave her on someone's doorstep to be cared for? I had such a friend who didn't wait for me to ask. She moved in with me and took care of my needs during my initial time of bereavement. I'm still in recovery. For over 50 years, I cared for others, now I needed care. The roles reversed.

I climbed out of that imaginary basket without realizing I needed to be nurtured and taken care of because of my emotional and mental injuries. Because of my instincts of a nurturer, I began functioning in a dysfunctional manner. Immediately, a familiar pattern evolved – diving into a work.

Because of my strong personality, no one stopped me and tapped me on the shoulder and said, you are bleeding. If you continue you are going to hemorrhage and become delusional because of the loss of blood, which is life. After seven years, the emotional bleeding has stopped. I spoke on this in Chapter 7 of this book. Remember, healing is a process. We must be obedient to the process.

It is so important to recognize that there are some episodes and seasons in our life where we feel we are not meeting goals, or that we're at a standstill; but, we must realize that we can redeem the time at any moment God has ordained. We can buy back opportunities we feel are gone. It starts with us.

Determine what season of life you are in and plan for interruptions. You can't; but, God is usually allowing events or things to interrupt our life journey, but for a reason. Our part is to stay on our faith journey; one day at a time. The Holy Spirit is the Seer. He will lead and guide us into all truth.

Getting to the heart of an interruption requires slowing down, trim all the needless or dispensable matter away from the heart, i.e. emotions, mind, as in circumcision. There must be a cutting away of the foreskin, that harbors and covers the inward parts of heart matter.

Fat can be used as an example. What is fat in the natural? Fat can smother the heart. It's a blocker in places where unhealthy tissue can live and attract unwanted debris. So, it is in the spirit realm. It can prevent your spirit from soaring and receiving life. It's that part of us that should be placed on the altar for cleansing.

In the Old Testament of the Bible, the fat was cut away from the sacrifice and placed in the fire. It would dissipate. Go up in a puff of smoke. There was no substance there. You can compare it with pride. It will dissipate, and then what remains? This is who we are.

As with emotional fat, we must remove ourselves from the unnatural wombs in our lives that we are still attached to. Our wombs might be fear of rejection, abandonment, low self-esteem, effect of secrecy, deception, lack of trust, victim mentality, relationships, past and future hurts and lack to name a few.

The umbilical cord must be cut so new life can emerge. It's comfortable staying attached to old bonds. You can't grow if you don't come out of the unnatural wombs of the past. Cords must be severed. Death can come from many sources. It would be the same as nutrients pulling from different organs and sucking out water or life.

The umbilical cord is the natural bloodline from the mother and the source of many things; some positive and some negative; some healthy and some unhealthy. The mother transfers and imparts many things to that infant in the womb. Her part is to nurture and impart. But, God has already designed the purpose and poured everything needed into that infant. That impartation can override any plan or scheme of the enemy for destruction: spirit, soul and body.

Once disconnected from the womb, either healthy or unhealthy nutrients (thoughts) can be transferred into the heart (spirit). Staying connected to the truth, through God's word, can transform you to avoid conforming to this world. On that path, Godly fruit is produced.

Keep thy heart with all diligence; for out of it are the issues of life.
Proverbs 4:23

Issues spoken of in this passage are extremities of borders, sources of life and escape from death.

Boundaries and borders must be established in our lives. It is our responsibility to guard and protect our hearts with due diligence for out of it flow the issues or sources of our life. Be aware of the affect cuts and bruises brought on by invasive surgeries, spiritually and physically. These processes can escalate from minor cuts and bruises to deep wounds of the heart.

When these deep wounds occur, radical surgery is necessary. The result is development of scar tissue. This tissue grows as a covering which is God's order of protection. It is at that time we must prepare ourselves for circumcision of the heart. The process is the same as natural circumcision spoken of in Genesis 17:10-14; 23-25.

The surgery is radical and bloody; but, necessary. It's a cutting away of the foreskin, or dead life choices, so new blood can flow in our hearts and lives. We must let go of dead works and thoughts that do not lead to life giving principles. The method is easy. Confront yourself. Ask the Holy Spirit to reveal truth. Ask him, what is the next step? The ultimate goal is to demonstrate what a circumcised heart looks like. Pure in the eyesight of God.

This chapter is an introduction to the first step to recovery from your personal setbacks. Your setback could be anything that has altered your natural development path: i.e. rape, incest, divorce, sudden tragedy – you put your face on the circumstance. The goal for all of us is recovery from that setback.

What two points were awakened in you as you read this chapter?

_____

_____

_____

_____

_____

_____

REFLECTIONS AND APPLICATION

Your reflection should include the following:

Which points had the most value to you?

What direct application can you use now in your life?

What else did you leave with after reading this chapter?

_____

_____

Chapter 2

THE PATH TO RECOVERY IS A PROCESS

We must recognize how God can change seasons in our lives instantaneously as illustrated in **Amos 9:13-15**

> **Behold, the days come, saith the Lord, that the plowman shall overtake the reaper, and the treader of grapes him that soweth seed; and the mountains shall drop sweet wine, and all the hills shall melt.**
>
> **And I will bring again the captivity of my people of Israel, and they shall build the waste cities, and inhabit them; and they shall plant vineyards, and drink the wine thereof; they shall also make gardens, and eat the fruit of them.**
>
> **And I will plant them upon their land and they shall no more be pulled up out of their land, which I have given them, saith the Lord thy God.**

Compare winter, summer, spring and fall to our lives. You can't plant in the dead of winter; your seed will become frozen. Life cannot come or bloom in a frozen heart or mind. You can become stuck in a season. A thawing out must occur. The land is fruitful in the ordained season it is in. Let's look at:

> **And he shall be like a tree planted by the rivers of water, that bringeth forth his fruit in his season; his leaf also shall not wither; and whatsoever he doeth shall prosper.**
> **Psalms 1:3**

How do you un-thaw your heart, so that life can flow out of it? The word of God says that out of our bellies shall flow living waters. The heart and the belly are the same. Out of our spirit,

19

is everything that we need to prosper and be prosperous in this land. Open yourselves up to the leading of the Holy Spirit in your lives. But, first we must recognize the season we're in and then the thawing out will occur.

Our natural order of seasons is that spring is the time for planting; summer is the time for resting; fall is the time for harvesting and winter is the time of seed lying dormant in the ground.

If you feel you are dormant in your life; indicators being no movement, your land is cold and unfruitful. Rest and know you are right where you are supposed to be in this season of your life. A time of preparation and processing must take place before a harvest of fruit manifests itself in the next season. Our part is to break up that fallow ground of the heart. Out of the heart flow the issues of life. According to Jeremiah 4:3-4, the Lord is instructing the men of Judah and Jerusalem to break up their fallow ground and sow not among thorns. He's saying circumcise yourselves to the Lord and cut away the foreskins of your heart. The cutting away of foreskins of your heart could be habits, routines, traditions or religion. All can cover or smother your spirit or heart.

The cutting away of habits, routines, traditions in my life was recognizing that I had developed habits. Some good and some not. Habits to mask or cover a wounded spirit. Who would say going to church, taking on assignments to further God's kingdom was not a good thing. But, we can pervert foreordained purposes of God if we are running and being busy because of emotional responses.

Immediately following the death of my husband, I was able to return to the church.

I hit the ground running. Every response to a request was yes. But, I found out that this was a defense mechanism of mine to avoid true intimacy with God and a place where we get our directions. Watch, any man or woman who doesn't want to go home at the end of their day. The home should be a place of solace and a place where God abides. We hear people say, I could just stay at the church 24/7. That is not balance. The home is the true church. The building structure of the church is where we worship corporately.

We must circumcise ourselves to the Lord. Cut away un-curtailed activities or habits that will not allow us to open ourselves up to God who is our true covering. Our part is to recognize counterfeit coverings over our hearts which is where the Holy Spirit abides. We are capable of God consciousness as the Holy Spirit reveals truth to us.

Fear of intimacy can be a hindrance; preventing you from hearing from God. First step to true relationships and intimacy in the natural is to develop intimacy with God.

Know the season of life you are in. ARE YOU STILL IN RECOVERY FROM YOUR SETBACK?

> **Although the fig tree shall not blossom, neither shall fruit be in the vines; the labor of the olive shall fail, and the fields shall yield no meat; the flock shall be cut off from the fold, and there shall be no herd in the stalls:**
>
> **Yet I will rejoice in the Lord, I will joy in the God of my salvation.**
>
> **The Lord God is my strength, and he will make my feet like hinds' feet, and he will make me to walk upon mine high places. To the chief singer on my stringed instruments.**
> ### Habakkuk 3:17-19

We can redeem the time at any season and at any crossroad of our lives.

Walk circumspectly, not as a fool or an unlearned person, redeeming the time. As we know, the days are evil that we now live in. The writer Apostle Paul, spoke of this in Ephesians 5:15-17. The key is understanding what the will of God is in our lives.

It takes only one moment to get a fresh perspective of where we are. We must yield to the direction of the Holy Spirit, who abides in us. The first step is realizing that you can begin again. You can go back to the first directions that God gave you, through the Holy Spirit. He's been with us all the time.

He's waiting for us.

He's waiting for us to stop re-infecting wounds of insecurities, such as rejection and abandonment. Our experiences may be different. Your definition of abandonment could be a mother or father who were missing physically in your life. Another person's challenge could be the experience of living in a house with biological parents, who could not see that you were suffering from emotional rejection and still consider yourself abandoned. The results are the same; wounds in the soul brought on by human error. How can that error be corrected in the natural? It can't. A healing must take place spiritually and then manifest itself in the physical.

Everything we need is aboard with the presence of the Holy Spirit who will lead and guide us in all truths. He's here, waiting to direct us. Our part, as stated in 2 Corinthians 10:5 is to cast down imaginations and every high thing that exalts itself against the knowledge of God and bringing into captivity every thought to the obedience of Christ.

If we continue dwelling on things we feel have kept us from moving forward, we allow our emotions or something we perceive as an offense, such as abandonment, keep us from moving forward.

That sounds wonderful. But, how do we do that? The beginning of the healing process is recognizing that you are in need of healing. We must do a reality check.

Out of the abundance of the heart, the mouth speaks. What have you been confessing. I'm sure that Jesus is Lord. Is he Lord over your spirit, soul and body? Our delight should be in the law of the Lord; and his law do we meditate on day and night. Are we thinking about him; are we casting down thoughts that come against his word.

Hurt, rejection, abandonment, blindness to our seasons in life, and being stuck in a place of un-fulfillment is not God. Are you operating in a place of un-forgiveness towards a mate, sibling, parent, child, or loved ones who are in the grave?

The healing process starts with forgiveness. Forgive yourself first and then go on to releasing forgiveness towards others. Let the healing begin.

Why no recovery yet?

Why then is not the health of the daughter of my people not recovered.

> **The harvest is past, the summer is ended and we are not saved. For the hurt of the daughters of my people am I hurt? I am black, astonishment has taken hold on me. Is there no balm in Gilead; is there no physician there? Why then is not the health of the daughter of my people not recovered.**

> **Jeremiah 8:20-21**

At that time in history a Savior had not manifested himself, figuratively, in the land. But, now deliverance has come through the Lord Jesus Christ. No longer are we in the wilderness, not knowing the way, without hope. He died, rose, ascended on high and sent us another comforter in the form of the Holy Spirt, our Seer who abides in us. He will lead and guide us into all truth through the word of God. Jesus is the answer.

Daughters, (term defining relationship with God); endearment, close to his heart in this passage in the old testament. In 3 John 2 it states, **"Beloved I wish above all things that thou may prosper and be in health, even as thy soul prospereth."**

Health in both the old and new testament can be defined as (*restoring to soundness; wholeness (literally or figuratively); health, made up, perfected.* Health is available, which is wholeness of Spirit, Soul and Body. I Thessalonians 5:23 states, "And the very God of peace sanctify you wholly; and I pray God your whole spirit and soul and body be preserved blameless unto the coming of our Lord Jesus Christ."

While recovery is in process, we must define what wholeness looks like.

We are a spirit being, first, clothed in a body which allows us to function in this earth as human beings and we possess a soul. It is the last component of our being, the soul, that most of us are challenged with. We can choose to live out or die to our purposes in this life.

In Jeremiah 8:20-21 it speaks of endearment and being close to God's heart.

First, as stated in Jeremiah 8, we must recognize we are in relationship with God. The term "daughter" in this old testament scripture describes our relationship with God as daughters. We are close to his heart. Daughter is a term of endearment, close to his heart. We can also interject son into this passage. 3 John 2 confirms that we are the beloved of God and he wants us whole and to be in health.

Beloved I wish (pray) above all things that thou mayest prosper and be in health, even as thy soul prospers.
3 John 2

God wants us to prosper in health and in our souls. We must first, be true to our emotions. Listen to your inner voice. If you hurt, you hurt. If you are grieving the loss of a loved one, recognize you are in a grieving process. Do not stuff your feelings or emotions. Believe God's word, of course, but, be true to your voice. If we live and move in him, we are intertwined; spirit soul and body. The soul is the seat of our emotions. It is in this realm that we deal with wounds and holes in our souls. Many wounds are self-inflicted. We're bleeding and don't even know it.

Ask the question. What does Health look like?

It is the sense of restoring to soundness; wholeness (literally or figuratively): health, made up, perfected.

Healing and restoration is part of that process. There are layers to the natural and physical healing process. First indicator in the natural is the blueness of the wound which identifies that there is a bruise in the fleshly parts of the body. This can be brought on by unnatural impressions which manifest themselves with a mark or bruise in or on the body. The same is true in our soul.

Frozen emotions can manifest themselves in drug and alcohol abuse, human trafficking, domestic violence, child abandonment; abuses of all kinds. Before the healing process can begin, the root of our emotional upheavals must be identified. When did you disconnect from the natural development stages of your life which is the root of emotional indicators.

Be honest and say, I didn't make a smooth transition from one development stage to the other in my life. And I am living out those results.

25

Healing of the soul begins with identifying the root of the wound. When did you withdraw and become introverted and stopped the natural order of developments. Prevention of transition can come at any stage of development. It could have occurred during early childhood, adolescence, as young adults or into our mature stations in life.

Healing of the physical and healing of the soul is the same process. Emotional wounds and bruises will be manifested by our behaviors, verbally and physically. Physical wounds and bruises will be visual and easy to identify. The healing or recovery process is the same.

The healing of many physical cuts, bruises and dysfunctions of the body can be corrected by radical surgeries and other invasive processes. So is the case with emotional hurts and wounds of the heart. As mentioned earlier, circumcision of the heart; the seat of our emotions must occur for transformation of the mind to begin the healing process of our soul.

Healing and restoration is a process. Be obedient to the process. In natural healing, tissue grows over the affected area as a covering. Scarring is a natural part of the healing process. Every wound result has some degree of scarring. The exception to this are animals with complete regeneration, which regrow tissue without scar formation.

In Proverbs 20:30, the Word says, *"The blueness of a wound cleanseth away evil: so, do stripes the inward parts of the belly."* Before restoration, cleansing must take place. Repentance first, then roots plucked out and then God will begin the healing process.

Hebrews 10:35 says for you to not cast away your confidence. We have the word of God as our blueprint which is based on the promises of God. Don't you cast away your confidence is a command and action sentence. We do the work and it starts in the mind.

Delusions can be sent or chosen by God or you may choose your own delusion. Why do you think God would send a delusion? One reason is if we were disobedient as described in Isaiah 66:4. He would go further and allow us to believe a lie as spoken of in 2 Thessalonians 2:10-11. All because we rejected the voice of the Seer, the Holy Spirit. And it can escalate and our conscience can be seared or unresponsive to God's direction.

We serve a loving God who has sent the Holy Spirit who leads and guides us into all truth. Without the filters and direction of the Holy Spirit, it's possible we can believe a lie.

The definition for Delusions – for our purposes in this book is a (device) false belief or hallucination. According to Strong's Exhaustive Concordance, the Hebrew translation for delusion is described as a fit coming on, i.e. vexation. In the Greek, delusion is described as a mental straying which shows itself in wrong actions and responses. This section is also addressed further in Chapter 4.

In Isaiah 66:4, the Lord said, *"I also will choose their delusions and will bring their fears upon them; because when I called, none did answer; when I spake, they did not hear; but they did evil before mine eyes, and chose that in which I delighted not."*

Also in 2 Thessalonians 2:10-11 it says that because they received not the love of the truth that they might be saved…for this cause, God shall send them strong delusion, that they should believe a lie.

We cannot mystify or spiritualize a delusion which is a false belief which we might develop ourselves or it can come from another source; even God. We are delusional if we believe that our development stages were all smooth transitions. Emotional abandonment can be based on not being invited to a social gathering as an adolescent. And when that occurs, again, in our adult life, it can open wounds in our soul and become a setback or interruption on our path to recovery.

If a delusion does occur in our minds, we must meditate on the word of God as stated in Psalms 1:2-3. And that man shall be like a tree planted by the rivers of water that bringeth forth his fruit in his season; his leaf shall not wither and whatsoever he doeth shall prosper.

God will chasten us to get our attention in all seasons of development and recovery; but, we know as spoken in Hebrews 12:11 that no chastening for the present seemeth to be joyous, but grievous, nevertheless afterward it yieldeth the peaceable fruit of righteousness unto them which are exercised thereby.

God will choose our delusions, only after we, willfully, reject his truth and choose our own path of delusion. We can't recover from a setback or interruption without repenting and getting back on our God ordained path for recovery.

Ask yourself these two questions.

Why is there no recovery from your setback yet?

Are you delusional in what you are imagining as recovery in your mind?

_____

_____

_____

_____

_____

REFLECTIONS AND APPLICATION

Your reflection should include the following:

Which points had the most value to you?

What direct application can you use now in your life?

What else did you leave with after reading this chapter?

Chapter 3

WHAT ARE THE SIGNPOSTS OF RECOVERY?

Dreams and visions are ignited when we come out of our asylum or hiding places. It's a natural thing to build walls around emotional hurts. We tend to guard our hearts as a defense mechanism. But, when recovery or restoration is imminent, our spirit and soul is awakened. Our excitement, zeal and passion about life is refueled. As a result, we exhibit those feelings in the natural places where we exist.

> **Behold the days come saith the Lord that the plowman shall overtake the reaper and the treader of grapes him that soweth seed; and the mountain shall drop sweet wine and all the hills shall melt.**
>
> **And I will bring again the captivity of my people Israel, and they shall build the waste cities, and inhabit them and they shall plant vineyards and drink the wine thereof; they shall also make gardens and eat the fruit of them.**
>
> **And I will plant them upon their land and they shall no more be pulled up out of their land which I have given them, saith the Lord thy God.**
>
> **Amos 9:13-15**

As the Lord is thawing us out and bringing us out of our places of complacency, we must be keenly aware by engaging the Holy Spirit who is our Seer and revealer. Many of us are naïve. Others can see and reveal truth to us that we thought was hidden based on our conversations and behaviors. When do we know that our hearts have been broken? Our behavior reveals our state of being. Indifference is a red flag that we are not being true to our emotions. Another sign is going through the motions of living; but, not excited about it.

Years ago, I had a health challenge. After the issue was corrected, my doctor shared that one of the indicators, to her, that my immune system and health had been compromised was that I didn't get excited when she mentioned my young grandchildren. She had all the clinical test results in front of her and confirmation of the medical diagnosis; but, the emotional part of me was frozen or stuck. This is indicated when we deviate from our ordained purposes and paths set apart by God. Interruptions come; but, are not permanent paths.

Hungering and thirsting for God's Word and righteousness is a way back to the Father and supping with him. Healing and restoration brings with it a true connection with God, his creation and a true hunger for the Word of God. In that excitement, we are grateful and appreciate our senses of tasting, feeling and truly seeing the work of God as he propels us into the places he has prepared for us. We become grateful and appreciate living again.

How do we go back to that Kairos moment and redeem what God has called us to do? What is your passion in life? What gets you excited and starts you to act and move and get unstuck? It's your God-given dream and vision. What did God instruct you to do in life and wrap yourself around? You can be faithful over another man's work and he will reward you for that work. He will also reward you for being obedient to what he has instructed you to do.

We can't pour all our wine and fruit from our vineyards on ourselves and those close to us.

Our dreams, visions and passions are to be shared with humanity as God allows us to come up out of our valleys of life. We are the repairers of the breached. But, the first place to start is within ourselves.

God said he would restore the old waste places of our life. What are waste places? These are the dumping grounds that, in many cases, we have created in our minds. That's the first place seeds of life fulfillments can be planted. If you think devastation, you can become and remain devastated. If you think fear, you can become fearful. But, God has not given us a spirit of fear but power, love and a sound mind. His word, revealed by the Holy Spirit, lets us see, feel and taste life. Stir up the gifts and passion God has given you for a successful journey in life as revealed in scripture in 3 John 2.

As God empowers, restores and allows us to build capacities, we can connect with and motivate others. We all have testimonies about our lives that brought us to the place that we are now. Not only the testimonies; but, many of us are in the rebuilding stages of our lives right now.

Abraham Maslow's Human Motivation Theory

Survival skills are imbedded in all human beings. We wonder many times what keeps us on our path. Self-actualization, or self-fulfillment, is a motivating factor. Before we can empower and assist others, we must reach our capacities in the soulish realm of life. That includes taking care of our human needs.

Abraham Maslow was an American psychologist who was known for his study of stages of human growth in humans. He used terms such as physiological, safety, belonging and love, esteem, self-actualization and self-transcendence which is no more than our God consciousness in which we are capable of seeing life and being directed by the Holy Spirit.

Maslow's hierarchy of needs is a motivational theory in psychology comprised of a five-tier model of human development needs; often depicted as hierarchical levels within a pyramid. Maslow stated that people are motivated to achieve certain needs. Our most basic need is for physical survival, and this will be the first thing that motivates our behavior. Once that level is fulfilled the next level up is what motivates us, and so on.

Those five-stage needs include:

Biological and physiological needs – air, food, drink, shelter, warmth, sex, sleep

Safety needs – protection from elements, security, order, law, stability, freedom from fear

Love and belongingness needs – friendship, intimacy, trust and acceptance, receiving and giving affection and love. Affiliating, being part of a group (family, friends, work).

Esteem needs – achievement, mastery, independence, status, dominance, prestige, self-respect, respect from others.

Self-Actualization needs – realizing personal potential, self-fulfillment, seeking personal growth and peak experiences.

The hierarchy of needs was expanded to include transcendence needs. According to Webster's definition means going beyond ordinary limits; surpassing; and exceeding.

Extending that which has been birthed out of your capacity to humanity in need must come from a desire to help build capacities in others. You can't motivate others if you haven't reached the place of self-actualization yourself.

Each one of our development stages brings us to the place of our personal capacity building.

Once capacity has been established and expanded in us, we can look at pouring out onto humanity what God has prepared us for in the marketplace of ministry. We are all ministers, which means servant. We have a work to take all that God has poured into us and pour into someone else.

As a signpost to our personal recovery from setbacks, we reignite visions, dreams, purposes and desires. All of this must be aimed at humanity. Not only are we being restored; but, we are pouring into someone else. An anecdote to our healing is evaluating which rung of the ladder we are on in our human development stages as described in Maslow's theory.

The stage of Self-Actualization must be achieved before moving to the next level. After a setback or interruption in our lives, you must reconnect with yourself and the vision, dream or purpose revealed to you when you started on your journey.

As I mentioned in 2011, my husband, Albert made his transition from life on earth to eternity with God after a sudden illness and departure. That was a set-back or interruption in my life. How did I recover? I'm still in recovery. I'm out of the intensive care unit (ICU); recovery is a process. Signposts of healing pop up along the way. The most prevalent is self-actualization. It's at this point, you can reach the highest goal in human development – reaching out to someone else and assist with their healing process. It's at that point you become a servant leader.

What two signposts to healing or recovery are you discovering after reading this chapter?

_____

_____

_____

How can you apply and pass on those discoveries to help build someone else's capacity for growth?

_____

_____

_____

REFLECTIONS AND APPLICATION

Your reflection should include the following:

Which points had the most value to you?

What direct application can you use now in your life?

What else did you leave with after reading this chapter?

Chapter 4

WHO IS THE SEER IN THIS LAND WE LIVE IN?

The Holy Spirit is the Seer or guide. He gives direction. Where do you get your directions? As a born-again believer, spoken of in John 3, we cannot even see or walk on a path to resolve many situations that occur in our lives without being born again and led by the Holy Spirit. One of my crossroads came in my adult life; married and with three daughters to raise.

Before my encounter with Jesus, I finally realized other people were not my problem. My bad attitude, inability to resolve conflicts, resolve family issues, growing up in a household where both parents, having seven children to raise, were not aware of my personal conflicts. After continuously directing my hostility onto others. I realized it was me with the unresolved issues; not them.

Two friends who I worked with, took me as their personal project. Despite my rejection of them, the Holy Spirit directed them to continue praying, continue reaching out in love, continue in their pursuit of winning my heart for Christ. The Holy Spirit took up residence in me as part of that package. That's why he is the Seer in this land.

It was at that point, I recognized who is available to guide my life. And that was Jesus Christ who I accepted as my Lord and Savior. But, even if you are not a born-again believer, I'm sure you have had occasion when you were at the cross roads of your life where you needed direction.

In Ephesians 5:14-15 we are encouraged to awaken and Christ shall give us light. The next step is that we walk circumspectly, not as fools, but as wise men and women; and redeem the time. Take advantage of every opportunity to recover from setbacks or interruptions in our lives.

I remind myself often that Christ died for me before I became a believer. In Romans 5:6-8, it speaks of the fact that while I was without strength, meaning that I needed direction, He died for me and left me a comforter and guide who is the Holy Spirit. The Holy Spirit is the teacher and will guide us in all truth.

Since we are talking about the works of the Holy Spirit and that He is the Seer in the earth, I can't help but go to the Book of Acts and look at His works through the Apostles. They were mere men, the same as us who had an assignment. What's your assignment in this life? To whom much is given, much is required. I'm not going to preach; but, I am going to teach because that's one of my assignments in this life. I know it's easier to stay in our man or woman made caves and just exist. It's easier. I challenge you, have you acknowledged the calling on your life. Each of us have different callings, purposes, assignments – label it whatever you choose.

But, have you started your journey?

The Holy Spirit is the Seer; but, he works through men and women of God whose gifts are used in many capacities in the church and in the true market place of the earth. And he gave some apostles and some prophets and some evangelists and some pastors and teachers for the edifying of the body of Christ...Those same men and women are called to go out into the market place, which is the world, to compel those who are lost to receive Jesus as their Lord and Savior.

Self-examination is in order. Have you been called to build a great cathedral or a housing complex for the less advantaged? Is your assignment to feed the hungry? Have you been called to be an evangelist and compel those who are lost to turn to Jesus Christ and be saved. Are you assigned to the field of education as a teacher, principal, or curriculum developer?

Or, is an entrepreneurial spirit haunting you?

Whatever the call or assignment, we must get busy and do the work. This chapter is designed to stir up the gifts within you with the help of the Holy Spirit. What is His specific role in our lives?

How to Steps on Engaging the Holy Spirit in our Assignments

We must engage truth and the role of the Holy Spirit in our lives. Here are a few steps on engaging the Holy Spirit and His role in accomplishing that necessary part that's needful in us for a successful journey. On that journey of life, we have the assurance of the Holy Spirit's presence in our lives if we have invited him in. The role of the Holy Spirit is that:

He gives directions
He counsels
He directs
He forewarns
He's available always because He abides in us
He comforts and consoles
He's smart; He has the intellect of God

You need people to accomplish goals and assignments. Loners accomplish very little in life. We cannot do it alone. Positive affirmations are necessary as we encourage ourselves and allow others to encourage us. What does networking look like to you? For me, it's taking the strengths and knowledge of others and gleaning from those in that inner circle before you enter the market place where true ministry is exhibited.

Do you have an inner circle is the first question? It's okay to acknowledge and let others in your inner circle know you have a vision in life. You can't birth the vision without assistance. While you are in the throngs of pain during the birthing process, who's attending to you. Who's identifying the signs of a successful delivery or a delivery that's being aborted?

41

Les Brown, a renown motivational speaker, stated that many times we go to our graves without fulfilling our dreams. Or better yet without fulfilling our purposes. We want to put a label on others as dream-killers. The truth is, we abort and kill our own purposes and dreams. It's called self-sabotage. We become delusional about who the enemy is and abort the birth of our own dreams. We are our own worst enemies. We don't need a how to on that. We've all been very successful in that abortion process of killing our dreams and aborting our purposes.

Pride is the underlying culprit in aborting our dreams and purposes. What's the image you have of yourself. Before we get out of control in our thought process which could rapidly escalate to suicidal tendencies, we must stop and redeem the time. How do you deescalate that process when you are mentally numb and unable to feel?

Wage a war on pride.

Pride goes before destruction, and a haughty spirit before a fall. Give those in your inner circle permission to speak into your life; especially in that space when you're too prideful to ask for and accept help. The Holy Spirit doesn't need permission because you allowed him to enter your life. He already has a carte blanc permission card. The key is to listen to the promptings of the Holy Spirit. He will enable those of your inner circle to speak truths to you.

Pride in your lineage can prevent you from revealing to others that you really don't have it all together. If your family was known for being high achievers, how can you reveal to others that you failed to accomplish low levels of self-actualization in your own lives and influenced the lives of your children. Take generational curses out of your vocabulary. Your Mom and Dad's standards do not define who you are and the purposes that God has predestined in your life. You have not cursed your children because of your perceived lack of accomplishments.

If that revelation is not enough, God wants us to demonstrate what the Apostle John has prayed; that we have a successful journey in life.

**Beloved, I wish above all things that thou mayest prosper and be in health even as your soul prospers.
3 John 2**

What does prospering look like to you? This Greek word for prosper means to have a successful journey of life; successful in business and in health; even as your soul prospers.

We are made up of spirit, soul and body. We are a spirit, we live in a body and we possess a soul. Who we are is manifested in those three elements which make up our being so we can function in this earth.

The heart is the seat of our emotions which is part of the soul. Included in our soul is the mind. We spoke earlier of keeping or guarding our hearts with all diligence because out of it flow the issues of life. We can say that the issues of the heart are life circumstances which many times interrupt or cause a setback in our conceived success plan.

Before any plan can be developed, we must first get the direction of the Seer; the Holy Spirit. Even if we acted prematurely by receiving a vision we thought was from God and began implementing without getting his instruction, we can redeem the time. Pause, ask for redirection from the Holy Spirit.

The key word is pause. Get unstuck, and then proceed.

We addressed pride as being a culprit in sabotaging the plan God has for us. Destructive behavior can come from within and usually originates in the thought process. Being caught up with how we are perceived by others can interrupt our life journeys. Be concerned about the wisdom others in your inner circle share; but, you don't want a stop and go journey because of others who are not part of your process.

We can agree that feeding the hungry is an admirable assignment; but, is it yours. There are so many ministries doing great things for the Kingdom of God; but, is it yours. One of Jesus' disciples asked about Apostle John, but, what about this man, Jesus answered, what's it to you if he tarries till I return. Jesus said, "You follow me". Basically, Jesus is saying stay on your water course or path.

We all must be about our Father's business. Hurry up and wait. Pause and get directions, daily, from the Holy Spirit. Our purpose and mission must be spirit lead and directed by the Holy Spirit. He is the seer. The Holy Spirit orchestrated the works of the Apostles in the Book of Acts. Each Apostle had varying gifts for their specific assignments.

How did the disciples respond in times of adversity? People are looking at how you respond to adversity. One of the Apostles, named Barnabus, whose name meant son of encouragement and reconciliation demonstrated what his name and gifting was. He assisted in resolving conflicts among his peers and others. And he also gave material gifts to those in need for a common cause. The Apostles and Disciples were bond together and had all things in common which included their possessions. He was used mightily by God. Referenced in Acts 4:36 and Acts 11.

Our part, with the help of the Holy Spirit, is to stir up the gifts God has bestowed upon us in matters of the heart whether in your family or in the market place. Interesting, when we speak of you stirring up the gifts that are in you; you may say that you are not called to preach, establish churches, teach people, and that you are not a leader. But, you are a leader. There's someone or a group of people that are watching how you respond to situations utilizing the gifts God has placed in you.

People are watching when things are not going well with you, personally; leaders are born or developed during times of personal attacks. How do you operate under pressure? How do you recover from setbacks or interruptions in life? What do you do when heroes are taken from you prematurely, family members disown you, husbands or wives divorce you without any warnings, parents favor one sibling above another and when people say all manner of evil against you.

That's when you call out to God and acknowledge, Lord I know you called me to this journey in life. God, what are the "how to's" in this situation. What self-help tool kit do you have for this situation pertaining to the heart. When we think or say things like this, we know God has a sense of humor because he already knows the plans and purposes he has for you. He knows exactly where you are and knows how he's going to rescue you at the right and appointed time.

I'm amazed at bible stories we've heard all our lives and the revelation that has been revealed at these times in our lives. It's at the time of intersect, when God meets the need at the appointed time and then gives direction as to what to do next that I'm in awe. I'm reminded of the story of Jonah in the bible. The Lord prepared a big fish (i.e. whale) to be in place and rescued Jonah when he was thrown overboard from the ship by the sailors on board. It's called positioning; being in the right place, at the right time, for rescue and recovery. I stay in awe of the all-knowing God.

The enemy wants to steal our joy and abort our God-given visions prematurely. He will attempt to steal our joy in matters of the heart; the seat of our emotions. An interruption or setback can be a fleeting moment or it can spill over into a lifetime. Recognize attacks of the enemy. He is the accuser of the brethren. He uses what you haven't done to taunt you.

Guilt

Guilt is one entrance into our thought pattern. What better way than guilt as an entrance can we be bombarded with the past. You can't stay in the past on what you could've and should've done in life. Those who are parents can relate to feeling that we didn't do enough in raising or training our children. There is a difference in raising and training. If we go back, we might look at the economics of their development; the lack of money.

A single mother of four, I knew from the past, was being challenged by her grown son. His charge to her was that his failure at age 40 was because she had to move the family to public housing when he was a teenager. She responded that her shoulders were broad; meaning I accept my responsibility. Not only will grown children blame parents for their challenges in life; but, we as parents, internally, accept that analysis of what went wrong in their grown children's lives was because of you. We in turn will carry that burden which is not ours to carry. Know this, you did the best you could do at that season of your life. Don't allow anyone to still your joy.

Guilt can interrupt or set back your vision implementation timelines if you allow it. Thinking about the past and what you haven't accomplished, can keep you from moving forward.

What do you do? You pause, ask the Holy Spirit, the Seer, to bring back to your remembrance the last thing God instructed you to do. When this is revealed, the log jam that keeps the flow of spiritual waters moving in our hearts is identified and can be unjammed or unstuck. The key word is pause, not "guilt", of what you didn't do; but, how do I get back on my water course or path.

The Holy Spirit is the revealer. He uses men and women of your inner circle to reveal truth to you. Stay in a place of receiving.

Self-Denial

Self-denial can keep us from hearing from others. Pride and guilt can become walls to our receiving a word that can propel us into the next level of our journey. Self-denial can contribute to our not moving forward. Not being truthful with ourselves for the cause of our delays can also contribute to delays. Readily admit when our pedagogy is untruths; which results in a foundation that will not sustain the vision God has given you.

God is about leading us to a multifaceted life of capacity building. The Holy Spirit leads and guides us into all truths; not false foundations based on our pride and guilt. There is no condemnation to those who are in Christ, who walk not after the flesh, but after the Spirit. Know when you get the victory for each battle that there will be many more battles, and many more victories...

Give God the Glory.

Based on what you have read in this chapter, who is the "Seer" in the land?

What is your definition of the function of the "Seer" in this land?

What's your part in the operation of the "Seer" and his work?

_____

_____

_____

_____

_____

_____

_____

REFLECTIONS AND APPLICATION

Your reflection should include the following:

Which points had the most value to you?

What direct application can you use now in your life?

What else did you leave with after reading this chapter?

Chapter 5

REDEEMING THE TIME FOR THE DAYS ARE EVIL

Hezekiah's Healing

There may have been many interruptions or setbacks in our lives; but, God continues to guide those He has called. As human beings, it's natural for us to want to see signposts or indications that God is confirming his word in our lives during our healing or recovery season.

King Hezekiah in 2 Kings 20:1-21 and 2 Chronicles 32:31 became ill. The prophet Isaiah came to Hezekiah and said, Hezekiah *"Set your house in order, for you shall die and not live."*

Hezekiah turned his face to the wall and cried out to God for his healing, with tears. He told God how he had been faithful; he pleaded with God to spare his life, with tears. God granted his request.

Walls are necessary when it's time to talk to God. We can't leave any space between God and our intimacy with him. As in marriage when a man and woman are joined together, they cleave to each other; there can be no space between them. We should even eliminate our own personal limited self-talk. We get God's attention when we do not allow anything else to enter in with us; that includes pride. Hezekiah was not too proud to beg God for his mercy. But, as you will see later in 2 Chronicles 32:31, pride entered his heart, "**God left him alone in order to test Hezekiah, to know what was in his heart**."

God already knew Hezekiah's deeds. But, he allowed him and will allow us to rehearse them so our faith can be built up. This is when we can buy opportunity, redeem the time and receive God's grace, one more time, a second time, a third time or as often is necessary.

In 2 Kings 20:4-5, this is demonstrated.

> **And it came to pass afore Isaiah was gone out into the middle court that the word of the Lord came to him, saying, Turn again, and tell Hezekiah, the captain of my people, thus saith the Lord, the God of David, thy father, I have heard thy prayer, have seen thy tears: behold, I will heal thee on the third day thou shalt go up unto the house of the Lord.**
>
> **And I will add unto thy days fifteen years; and I will deliver thee and this city out of the hand of the king of Assyria; and I will defend this city for mine own sake, and for my servant David's sake."**
>
> **And Isaiah said, "Take a lump of figs, and they took and laid it on the boil, and he recovered."**
>
> **And Hezekiah said unto Isaiah, "What shall be the sign that the Lord will heal me, and that I shall go up into the house of the Lord the third day?"**
>
> **And Isaiah said, "This sign shalt thou have of the Lord, that the Lord will do the thing that he hath spoken: shall the shadow go forward ten degrees, or go back ten degrees?"**
>
> **And Hezekiah answered, "It is a light thing for the shadow to go down ten degrees; nay, but let the shadow return backward ten degrees."**
>
> **And Isaiah the prophet cried unto the Lord: and he brought the shadow ten degrees backward, by which it had gone down in the dial of Ahaz.**

Isaiah, the prophet, gave him a choice. He said this is the sign to you from the Lord, that the Lord will do the thing that He has spoken. This example, for our purposes in this book, is the illustration of the Sun Dial of Ahaz for measuring time. Isaiah asked Hezekiah, if the shadow should walk forward ten steps or go back ten steps? Hezekiah answered that it is an easy thing for the shadow to stretch ten steps, so let it go back ten steps. Hezekiah wanted a sign that couldn't be questioned.

After Hezekiah's healing, scripture says. Hezekiah got caught up in pride. In Chapter 4, we talked about how pride cometh before a fall and a haughty spirit before destruction. God already knew He allowed the Assyrians to come into his palace, home, where all his hidden treasures of God were and see everything. He got caught up in pride and wanted to boast of his possessions and God's treasury. That's why God left him to try him that he might know all that was in his heart.

Your journey is a time of testing by God who already knows the outcome.

Your Healing And Recovery From Setbacks

Our processes in obtaining healing and total recovery requires us to walk circumspectly, or watch our steps, according to Ephesians 5:15-16 and Colossians 4:5 *See, then that you walk circumspectly, not as fools but as wise, Redeeming the time because the days are evil.* We can help others and exhibit wisdom toward them by watching our steps and getting an understanding on how to obtain our healing and recovery from setbacks by redeeming the time and taking advantage of opportunities that arise.

In this same passage it says to *walk in wisdom toward them that are without, outside, redeeming the time.* Your journey is a time of testing by God who already knows the outcome. Part of our healing and recovery is to enable and assist someone else in completing their human development stages mentioned in Chapter 3 (Maslow's Theory).

In Daniel 2:8, Daniel also speaks of redeeming the time. King Nebuchadnezzar gave Daniel and the other wise men an opportunity to redeem their lives by revealing and interpreting his dream. If they were not able to reveal the king's dream and interpret it, he would have them killed. As a demonstration, he had already had many of them slain because they couldn't reveal the dream. His statement to them was:

I know of a certainty that you would gain the time, because the thing has gone from me.

The term redeem or gain the time is illustrated here in Ephesians, Colossians and again in Daniel 2:8 meaning: Ye are gaining or protracting time. These illustrations are similar. In Colossians 4:5 redeeming the time is by prudent and blameless conduct, gaining as much time and opportunity as possible in view of persecution and death.

It generally means to buy up, to buy all that can be bought not allowing a suitable moment to pass unheeded.

Redeeming the time. Opportune time (Kairos), opportunity; however, implies not the convenience of the season, but the necessity of the task at hand whether the time provides a good, convenient opportunity or not; times at which certain foreordained events take place or necessary accomplishments need to take place.

We cannot wait for the opportune and convenient time to be a part of our own recovery and healing. It's necessary to do the task at hand. How to do that is to remind ourselves to look at the vision, purpose, assignment God has given you. Seek the direction of the Seer in the land, who is the Holy Spirit and complete the task at hand. You've already written the vision down; it's plain to you; now do the work. He's a God of many chances. And he's a rewarder of those who diligently seek him.

Many times, we leave space between God and us, as we give into our emotions and self-talk. We get puffed up, looking at our own good works. What do you do when there are no signs and wonders, when God does not appear to be there. And there's no visible cloud following us on our journey, no burning bush, no audible voice. This is the time of testing, as in the case of King Hezekiah:

God left him to try him that he might know all that was in his heart. (2 Chronicles 32:31)

It's in this moment, we redeem the time. Walk circumspectly, redeeming the time. Self-examination is always in order.

A little history application and warning for us in this day is to look at the Assyrians in Chapter 2 of Daniel. The Assyrians were foreigners in Israel and did not fear the God of the land. Though they did not fear God, He caused lions to come through the land and kill a few of them. He got their attention. They realized they had to learn how to worship God and reverence him.

The Assyrians took a priest of Israel who was in captivity and had him teach the rituals of worship, but they still erected their personal idols. He taught the foreigners of Assyria their customs. They feared God but served their own gods, after the manner of the nations whom they carried away.

They did not become acclimated to the voice of the Lord. They became acclimated to the culture of the land. In our case, God is interested in much more than outward conformity to his word and commandments. He wants circumcised and attentive hearts so he can bring forth the pre-ordained destiny and the path He has established in our lives. Our part is to Redeem the Time.

Would God leave you alone and be silent when you need an answer?

What would be the purpose?

What does redeem the time mean to you?

How does the term redeem the time apply to a present-day situation in your life?

What is that opportune time in your life?

_____

_____

_____

_____

_____

_____

REFLECTIONS AND APPLICATION

Your reflection should include the following:

Compare being acclimated into the culture of the world as opposed to following a pure circumcised and attentive heart towards God.

What are the benefits?

What direct application can you use now in your life?

What else did you leave with after reading this chapter?

_____

_____

_____

_____

_____

_____

_____

Chapter 6

HOW TO RECOVER – NEXT STEP

Daughters, you are the beloved of God. Is there no balm in Gilead? Is there no physician. Yes, there is a balm and yes there is a physician in your land. Gilead becomes our spirit, soul and body (land) today.

We started the journey of this book, Redeeming the Time - *How to Recover from Setbacks,* with discussion around a question. "**Is there no balm in Gilead**". The reason why this question was asked is because of a statement in Jeremiah 8:20-21. "My daughters are not yet saved."

Many of us have not been saved or delivered from those things that have prevented our restoration or recovery from setbacks in life. In Jeremiah, he speaks of a balm which is described in Hebrew as a kind of balm or salve; a medicine. Jeremiah 8:11 states that "my daughters are slightly healed from their hurts". But, our desire is a total recovery from setbacks and interruptions in our lives. A return to health which is restoration and soundness of spirit, soul and body.

By the ultimate sacrifice of Jesus Christ on Calvary have his daughters and sons been restored to soundness. It's been done through Jesus Christ. We must set our affections on things above and not on things in this earth, looking unto Jesus the author and finisher of our faith.

He's already abiding in us in the presence of the Holy Spirit. Everything we need for recovery is present within us. Everything you have gone through, personally, in life matters. God has allowed setbacks and interruptions in your life. Satan can only afflict or interrupt what God has allowed.

What does soundness look and feel like. The mind is the beginning of our thought patterns. Imaginations are our thoughts. In scripture it says that we can be transformed by the renewing of our minds. Transformation in our thought patterns can come by pausing and setting our emotions and affections on the things that are above and not on things in the earth or what has occurred in our lives. The power is seated on the right hand of God and in us in the presence of the Holy Spirit.

Pause for a moment. Remember Stephen, one of Christ's first martyrs in the Book of Acts. As they stoned him, he paused and looked up and saw Jesus, standing, beside God, on his throne. That was and still is Christ's position on the throne. You want to pause and look on him. Jesus is mobile, He's in all things. He's in a position of authority. He sends forth his angels to do his bidding on our behalf.

There is a 12-Step program which gets us back to recovery. We can't remain stuck or frozen in our quest for life.

The First step, is to Pause and get direction from the Holy Spirit, who is the Seer in the land (the land in this case, being you).

The Second step is use what is available to you, your full armor of God described in Ephesians chapter 6.

The Third step is knowing of a certainty that the vision and purposes God has ordained in your life is doable.

The Fourth step is knowing your own vision. Look at it daily. You should also know the plans God has for you. Keep it before your face. Whatever you call it: blueprint or vision board; make sure you have written it down. Keep your vision before you.

The Fifth step is commit to the vision and be obedient to the process; no matter how long it takes to manifest.

The Sixth step is to be in health even as your soul prospers. In 3 John 2 the word of God speaks of a successful journey. And part of that journey is to prosper in your health realm. Be healthy. Just as we are told to be holy for Jesus is holy. Be healthy. Take care of your physical temple.

The Seventh step is to know the voice of the Holy Spirit; don't move forward on impulse or emotions. Know his voice, know how to discern his voice. Confirm it in the Word of God.

The Eighth step is self-examination. Self-examination is always in order. Ask, what's my motivation for doing what I feel is part of this vision.

The Ninth step is to stay in contact with your inner circle of people. That's your safe group. Your first intimate group is with the Father, his son Jesus and the Holy Spirit, who are one.

The Tenth step is to be ready. What does readiness look like to you? You know the weights that keep you from running your race and moving in the direction of the vision God has given you. Lay them aside. Be ready to move with haste as the Holy Spirit gives direction.

The Eleventh step is Execute. What's the first thing God said for you to do. Each person's instructions are different. Are you to feed the poor, write a letter, give a word of encouragement to someone, or clean up the clutter in your life before moving forward. It could be as simple as asking someone to forgive you. That someone could be you.

The Twelfth step is to Redeem the Time. You can come full circle instantaneously in each area of your life. You can gain the time and make full proof of your ministry (serving in God's Kingdom); God's market place is the world.

When we quote Jeremiah, let your land be your place of reckoning, be your Gilead. There is a balm and there is a physician in the land. Your recovery process came about during the times of interruptions or setbacks. Your alabaster box was cracked open, your balm was leaked out. The box had to be cracked. The pressure had to be allowed so the balm could be leaked.

It was the anointing that came on your life which is leading you to recovery. Bask in the anointing of the balm. Let every crevice of your spirit, soul and body be lubricated so you can run when you read and hear the plain vision God has ordained on your life.

Chapter 6 – Summary

Are you prepared to implement the 12-Step Program to Recovery and redeem the necessary time?

Are you in health, even as your soul prospers?

What does recovery and health look like to you?

_____

_____

_____

_____

_____

_____

_____

_____

_____

REFLECTIONS AND APPLICATION

Your reflection should include the following:

Which points in this chapter had the most value to you?

What direct application can you use now in your life?

What else did you leave with after reading this chapter?

_____

_____

_____

_____

_____

_____

_____

_____

_____

_____

_____

Chapter 7

The Family

Just discovered...

My inner circle are my daughters: Kelly, Khadijah and Nisa.

Each one of my daughters are special in their assignments in my life. Impartations into not only my life; but, the lives God has given to them to be wise stewards over, their own children.

Kelly flipped the script. Her name means war, lively, aggressive. She's the oldest; but, has the two younger children, Jason and Jeremiah. The definition of her name describes her children. How else is she able to raise and train up these two zealous young men? They complement and reflect who she is. And she still has at least 10-15 more years to go in completing that process.

I'm so blessed that I, too, am still on her radar. She's my prayer partner and special covering in my life.

My second and middle daughter, Khadijah's name means precocious...before her time, wisdom. She knows. Eyes always full of excitement. One who honors her parents in the Lord. Very kind, very respectful, even when I'm wrong; she still smiles sweetly. But, has never rebuked this elder one. She is the one who left home at 22 years old; but, still honored a curfew before she left home. She did and still knows how to honor her Mama. When I want to vent and send those around me to hell, she gently brings the other person's positive side to the light. Bottom line, she just loves me out of my darker moments. She is creative and artsy, if there's such a word.

Her three children, Adrien, Marcus and Haile (aka Kareem) are true reflections of their Mom and Dad. They have received the impartation of respect and honor to their elders from their parents. She brings her artsy and creative part as my covering. She makes me laugh.

My third and youngest daughter Nisa's name means woman. She's everybody's mama, including me; full of wisdom, knowledge and understanding. During previous health challenges, she's the one who had the voice to insist on a doctor's visit. Her biological sons, Robert and Michael received her impartation. They know how to think outside the box.

She's one who knows how to release herself and release others. She knows how to cut her losses and move forward. She knew how women were to be covered and how to be covered.

As I look at my inner circle, which I discovered are my daughters, it's an opportunity for me to mirror who and what they are. And springboard into the next season God has given me. It is with honor that I receive these ladies as my inner circle. They give me strength; they make me proud.

Not only are they my support group, they also demonstrate common core values in their lives. Those values were imparted through the family. How important is the Family? Family is everything, after God. The traditional family structure may have changed; but, it remains your most important support group.

It's there that you develop your common core values. It is where you live and grow up. This is where character is built. What better place than the home are leaders developed. Parents as authority figures in the home demonstrate good or bad leadership qualities. In certain seasons of your life you may become your own parent and authority figure. You determine your successes in life.

John Bradshaw, a Christian psychologist, in his book, *Home Coming – Reclaiming and Championing Your Inner Child,* suggested as an exercise that we switch roles of parent and child. He had the readers to write a letter from the parent you felt had failed you. He suggested that you write it with your left hand if you are right handed. That shows the frailty of the child at that time. Instead of feeling slighted or operating in un-forgiveness, release yourself and you become the parent that you needed at that time. In that letter, say all the things you desired and needed to hear from that parent.

We cannot get stuck in a development stage and not become whole for the journey. We must speak into our own lives. Leaders are raised and trained in the home where common core values are the nucleus for development. Some of those values are honesty, integrity, dependability, emotional strength, capacity for vision and last, but not least, discipline and consistency.

Vision resonates in me as the beginning after recovery from setbacks. First, do you have a vision or dream? Have you allowed yourself to imagine what you would truly like to do in life? What is your passion? What is it you love to do and get excited about? Begin that journey at all cost. Look at what it will take to finish.

Success builds strong character because it is a journey of failures and successes. Strong character is built under pressure as you move toward personal goals. As leaders, we must prepare for the journey of success.

NOTES

INTRODUCTION

Kairos – Definition, also described in Chapter 3 - Kairos is a Greek word defined in Strong's Exhaustive Concordance as an opportune time (Kairos), opportunity; however, implies not the convenience of the season, but the necessity of the task at hand whether the time provides a good, convenient opportunity or not. These are times at which certain foreordained events take place or necessary accomplishments need to take place.

CHAPTER 1 – How to Recover from Upheavals in this Life and Regain Control After a Sudden Change or Disruption

Proverbs 4:23

Keep thy heart with all diligence; for out of it are the issues of life.

Genesis 17:10-14; 23-25 – Circumcision. Cutting away of Foreskin
...vss. 23-25 – Figurative Illustration of Circumcision of the Heart.

And Abraham took Ishmael his son, and all that were born in his house, and all that were bought with his money, every male among the men of Abraham's house; and circumcised the flesh of their foreskin in the selfsame day, as God had said unto him.

CHAPTER 2 – The Path to Recovery is a Process

Delusions – For our purposes in this book a delusion (device) is a false belief or hallucination. According to Strong's Exhaustive Concordance, the Hebrew translation is described as a fit coming on, i.e. vexation. In the Greek translation delusion is described as a mental straying which shows itself in wrong actions and responses.

Isaiah 66:1-4

Thus saith the Lord, The heaven is my throne, and the earth is my footstool: where is the house that ye build unto me? And where is the place of my rest?

For those things hath mine hand made, and all those things have been, saith the Lord: but to this man will I look, even to him that is poor and of a contrite spirit and trembleth at my word.

He that killeth an ox is as if he slew a man, he that sacrificeth a lamb, as if he cut off a dog 's neck; he that offereth an oblation as if he offered swine's blood; he that burneth incense, as if he blessed an idol. Yea, they have chosen their own ways, and their soul delighteth in their abominations.

I also will choose their delusions and will bring their fears upon them; because when I called, none did answer; when I spoke, they did not hear; but they did evil before mine eyes, and chose that in which I delighted not.

2 Thessalonians 2:11

"And for this cause God shall send them strong delusion, that they should believe a lie."

I Timothy 4:2

"Speaking lies in hypocrisy; having their conscience seared with a hot iron;"

Habakkuk 3:17-19

Although the fig tree shall not blossom, neither shall fruit be in the vines; the labor of the olive shall fail, and the fields shall yield no meat; the flock shall be cut off from the fold, and there shall be no herd in the stalls:

Yet I will rejoice in the Lord, I will joy in the God of my salvation.

The Lord God is my strength, and he will make my feet like hinds' feet, and he will make me to walk upon mine high places. To the chief singer on my stringed instruments.

Psalms 1:3

And he shall be like a tree planted by the rivers of water, that bringeth forth his fruit in his season; his leaf shall not wither; and whatsoever he doeth shall prosper.

CHAPTER 3 - What are the Signposts of Recovery

Kairos – Kairos – Definition, also described in Chapter 3 - Kairos is a Greek word defined in Strong's Exhaustive Concordance as an opportune time (Kairos), opportunity; however, implies not the convenience of the season, but the necessity of the task at hand whether the time provides a good, convenient opportunity or not. These are times at which certain foreordained events take place or necessary accomplishments need to take place.

Abraham Maslow Theory – Human Development Stages

Amos 9:13-15

Behold the days come saith the Lord that the plowman shall overtake the reaper and the treader of grapes him that soweth seed; and the mountain shall drop sweet wine and all the hills shall melt.

And I will bring again the captivity of my people Israel, and they shall build the waste cities, and inhabit them and they shall plant vineyards and drink the wine thereof; they shall also make gardens and eat the fruit of them.

And I will plant them upon their land and they shall no more be pulled up out of their land which I have given them, saith the Lord thy God.

Psalms 1:3

And he shall be like a tree planted by the rivers of water, that bringeth forth his fruit in his season; his leaf also shall not wither; and whatsoever he doeth shall prosper.

CHAPTER 4 – Who Are the Seers in this Land We Live In?

Seer – The Holy Spirit is the Seer. One who leads and guides. He reveals truth to all who will receive. He leads and guides us in all truth as stated in John 16:13

John 16:13

Howbeit when he, the Spirit of truth, is come, he will guide you into all truth: for he shall not speak of himself; but whatsoever he shall hear, that shall he speak: and he will shew you things to come.

Ephesians 5:14-15 and Colossians 4:5

Wherefore he saith, Awake thou that sleepest, and arise from the dead, and Christ shall give thee light. See then that ye walk circumspectly, not as fools, but as wise, Redeeming the time, because the days are evil.

Walk in wisdom toward them that are without, redeeming the time.

Les Brown – Minister of the Gospel, acclaimed author, motivational speaker, television personality, award winning speaker. Interest in self-education.

3 John 2

Beloved I wish above all things that thou mayest prosper and be in health even as your soul prospers

A delusion (device) is a false belief or hallucination.

CHAPTER 5. – Redeeming the Time for the Days are Evil

Redeem the time - Buy Opportunity

Kairos Moment - The word Kairos is a Greek word which means opportune time (kairos), opportunity; however, implies not the convenience of the season, but the necessity of the task at hand whether the time provides a good, convenient opportunity or not.

Ephesians 5:15-16, Colossians 4:5

Wherefore he saith, Awake thou that sleepest, and arise from the dead, and Christ shall give thee light. See then that ye walk circumspectly, not as fools, but as wise, Redeeming the time, because the days are evil.

Walk in wisdom toward them that are without, redeeming the time.

Daniel 2:8 ….know of certainty that ye would gain the time…

2 Kings 20:1-6

In those days was Hezekiah sick unto death. And the prophet Isaiah the son of Amoz came to him, and said unto him, Thus saith the LORD, Set thine house in order; for thou shalt die, and not live.

Then he turned his face to the wall, and prayed unto the LORD, saying, I beseech thee, O LORD, remember now how I have walked before thee in truth and with a perfect heart and have done that which is good in thy sight. And Hezekiah wept sore.

And it came to pass afore Isaiah was gone out into the middle court, that the word of the LORD came to him, saying, Turn again, and tell Hezekiah the captain of my people, Thus saith the LORD, the God of David thy father, I have heard thy prayer, I have seen thy tears: behold I will heal thee: on the third day thou shalt go up unto the house of the LORD. And I will add unto thy days fifteen years; and I will deliver thee and this city out of the hand of the king of Assyria; and I will defend this city for mine own sake, and for my servant David's sake.

2 Chronicles 32:31

Howbeit in the business of the ambassadors of the princes of Babylon, who sent unto him (Hezekiah) to inquire of the wonder that was done in the land, God left him, to try him, that he might know what was in his heart

CHAPTER 6 – How To Recover – Next Step

Jeremiah 8:20-21

The harvest is past, the summer is ended, and we are not saved.

For the hurt of the daughter of my people am I hurt; I am black; astonishment has taken hold on me.

Is there no balm in Gilead; is there no physician there? Why then is not the health of the daughter of my people not recovered.

Jeremiah 8:11..."my daughters are slightly healed from their hurts

Referenced Authors/Books

The Holy Bible – King James Version
Strong's Exhaustive Concordance – for Definitions in Hebrew or Greek

Webster's Collegiate Dictionary

John Bradshaw – Christian Psychologist. Author of Homecoming – Reclaiming and
   Championing Your Inner Child

Devotional – Beside the Still Waters – March, April 2018 Edition

Jentezen Franklin, Author, Right People, Right Place, Right Plan – formatting only

Robert Morris, Frequency, - formatting only

Made in the USA
Lexington, KY
28 November 2018